W9-CES-662

# Object Lessons About God

# Object Lessons About God

## Kyle Godsey

**BAKER BOOK HOUSE**
Grand Rapids, Michigan 49516

Copyright © 1991 by Kyle Godsey

Published by Baker Books
a division of Baker Book House Company
P.O. Box 6287, Grand Rapids, MI  49516-6287

ISBN: 0-8010-3841-3

Fourth printing, October 1994

*Printed in the United States of America*

To

my **family**

for a lifetime of love
and encouragement

# Contents

# Foreword

When I was appointed to be the Senior Minister at the Wickline United Methodist Church in Midwest City, Oklahoma, I was told about the wonderful children's sermons that were a part of the morning worship service. I soon discovered the truth of those words.

Week in and week out Kyle Godsey presents the gospel of Jesus Christ to the children of this congregation. His ability to catch a glimpse of the gospel in the objects that surround our everyday life is truly a gift. Kyle's insights into the life and mind of a child enable him to communicate the gospel in a way that children can easily understand and enjoy. In fact, he does such a good job that even the adult members of the congregation find his children's sermon to be a high point of worship. Since I have the best seat in the house, I get to see the smiles and nods of understanding on the faces of everyone in the sanctuary.

In this book you will find clear and helpful lessons that will make the children's moment, the Sunday school lesson, and any other teaching time with children, interesting and meaningful. As you use these object lessons in your church, watch the children respond as they begin to understand the depth and richness of God's grace. Kyle's calling and love of children is evident. I count it my privilege to have him as my friend, as well as the minister to the youth and children at our church. Read, use, and enjoy his creative work in this book.

Kent Ingram

# 1

# My Friend Clyde

**Key Point:** No matter how many kind words we share with others, unkind words still hurt.

**Objects:** Large, round balloon named "Clyde," and a straight pin

**Scripture:** Psalm 34:13; Psalm 39:1; Matthew 5:22; James 3:9–10.

**Preparation:** Blow up a large, round balloon. Place a five-inch piece of wide, clear packing tape across one side of the balloon. Keep this side of the balloon facing you throughout the message.

Hello! I'm really glad to see you! I've brought a friend with me and his name is "Clyde." [*Hold up the balloon.*] Clyde and I have been good friends for about three or four minutes now, and I'd like to share some words with him. I have a pin which represents the words I'm going to stick Clyde with. First, I'm going to stick Clyde with some kind words: "Clyde, you are the nicest balloon I know."

[*Stick the pin through the tape, then pull it back out. The balloon will not pop as long as you do this.*] Well, what do you know, these kind words didn't hurt Clyde at all. Let's try it again: "Clyde, I really like you." [*Stick the pin through the tape again.*] Hey, I think he likes being stuck with kind words. Let's say one more nice thing to Clyde: "Clyde, I'm glad you're my friend." [*Repeat the process.*] I wonder what would happen if I were to stick Clyde with some bad words: "Clyde, you're one big dummy!" [*Stick the balloon away from the tape, so it will pop.*] (Pop!) Hmmm, you would think after sticking him with so many good words, the bad words wouldn't hurt Clyde so much, but they did. People are a little like Clyde. No matter how many times we say something nice to someone, mean words still hurt. It's really important for us as Christians to try very hard to avoid saying unkind things to others.

*Dear God,*
*We know kind words make people feel good, but unkind words hurt more. Please help us to keep from saying unkind things to others. Amen.*

# 2

# An Act of Kindness

**Key Point:** God wants us to be kind to others.

**Object:** Picture of a wishing well

**Scripture:** Ephesians 4:32; Proverbs 11:17; Ruth 2:13; Mark 12:31.

**Preparation:** Draw a picture of a well or find a picture and paste it on a piece of posterboard.

Does anyone know what this is? This is a well: not an ordinary well, but a wishing well. Have you ever been to a wishing well? What do you do there? [*Allow for a few responses.*] That's right: you close your eyes, toss in a coin, and make a wish.

When I look at this picture I think of a story about two little girls. One day they went with their family to a large department store. Their mother gave the older girl two coins to toss into a wishing well that was located in the middle of the store. As she was just about to toss the coins into the well, the older girl stopped, turned to her younger sister, handed her one of the coins and said, "Here, you make a wish, your wishes are important too." Wasn't that a kind thing to do? This story tells a very important lesson about being Christians. Kindness is very important to God. Jesus tells us that one of the most important laws for Christians is to "love your neighbor. . . ." We do this by being kind and letting our neighbors know they are important. When we are kind, we make others feel good, and we even feel good ourselves.

*Dear God,*
*Thank you for all the kind things you've done for us and please help us to be kind to others. Amen.*

# 3

# No Time to Be A Christian

**Key Point:** God expects us to be Christians every day, not just when we can find the time.

**Objects:** Bag of candy and a very disheveled youth minister

**Scripture:** Joshua 24:15; Psalm 61:8; Luke 9:23.

**Preparation:** Arrange for an assistant to "fill in" during your absence at the beginning of the children's story. Have this person give you a cue when to come in like: "(Name)'s supposed to be here; I wonder where he/she is."

(Pastor) "Well, good morning . . . uh, hmmm . . . Kyle's supposed to be here this morning, I wonder where he is." [*Come rushing in, disheveled and carrying shoes in one hand and a bag of candy in the other.*] Whew, good morning! Oooh . . . let me catch my breath. Wow . . . I almost didn't make it today. I had so many things to get done this morning. I had to do my laundry, feed my cat, wash some dishes, call my parents and a lot of other things. I've been so busy I haven't had enough time to put together a little sermon for you. But don't worry, I had this extra bag of candy at home and I'll give each of you a piece of it if you'll let me off the hook today. I promise I'll have a wonderful story for you next week, okay? [*Start handing out the candy.*] Is this all right with everyone? (Undoubtedly, a few will say "No" just to be difficult.) No? Why not? Do you expect me to have a sermon for you every Sunday? (Undoubtedly, a few will say "Yes!" just to be difficult.) You do, huh? Well, okay, I think I have something I can share with you. Have you ever noticed we sometimes treat God like this? We get so busy in our daily lives that we say "God, I'm too busy to be a Christian today. I just can't take the time to be nice to anyone. If you let me take care of only myself today, I'll be twice as friendly to others tomorrow, okay?" What do you think God's response would be? He would say, "No, it's not okay." You see, if we say we are Christians, God expects us to be Christians every day of our lives. God wants us to take time every day to share his love with others.

*Dear God,*
*Please help us to be the kind and caring people you want us to be every day, even when we are busy. Amen.*

# 4

---

# Joyful Noise

**Key Point:** When we sing in church, we are singing to God; and no matter how we sing, God thinks it's beautiful.

**Object:** Song book

**Scripture:** 2 Samuel 22:50; Psalm 98:4; Ephesians 5:19; James 5:13.

**Preparation:** None

How are you today? I have a song book just like the ones in our church pews. [*Hold song book up for all to see.*] The song book is very important because it contains many wonderful songs we sing at each worship service. How many of you enjoy singing in church? How many of you feel kind of silly singing in church? Well, when I was your age I did not like to sing at all, especially in church. I used to sit with my dad in church and he didn't sing too well, or at least it didn't sound right to me. He would sing words wrong or even lose his place, and my friends and I would giggle at him. Then I started thinking, "If I mess up like this, my friends will laugh at me too." So I decided not to sing in church. Well, one Sunday morning when everyone else was singing, I started looking through my song book [*flip through the pages*] and I noticed many of these songs had something odd at the end of them. That something was the word *Amen*. Do you know what else ends with "Amen?" (Some child should say "Our prayers.") That's right, we end our prayers with "Amen." Some songs are also prayers. Then I realized my father didn't care what I or anyone else thought of his singing, because he wasn't singing to us, he was singing to God. The songs we sing in church tell God how much we appreciate him, love him, and need him in our lives; and no matter how loud, soft, good, or bad we sing, it's all beautiful to God. So when we get ready to sing our songs this morning remember whom we're singing to and how much he appreciates it.

*Dear God,*
*Thank you so much for the gift of singing. It is such a special way to praise you. In Christ's name we pray. Amen.*

# 5

# Thank You, God
## (Christmas Season)

**Key Point:** It is important that we take time to thank God for all he's given us.

**Objects:** "Thank You" lists

**Scripture:** 1 Chronicles 16:8; Job 37:14; Ephesians 5:20; Colossians 4:2.

**Preparation:** Prepare some colorful copies of the "Thank You" list prior to the service. Have an assistant available to help in handing out lists.

How many of you are ready for Christmas? Are you excited about all of the wonderful gifts you might get? I remember I used to make a "wish" list each Christmas and I would send it to my grandparents. I would wish for things like a fire truck, a baseball mitt, lots of games, and also candy. How many of you have already made up a Christmas "wish" list? [*Wait for a show of hands.*] Nearly every one of you. How many of you have made up a Christmas "thank you" list? Yes, a "thank you" list. You know, this time of the year we usually get so caught up in wishing for things we don't have, we forget to thank God for all of the wonderful things he has already given us. I made up a little "thank you" list for God and I would like to share it with you today:

*Dear God,*
*I would like to thank you for [Read from a copy of the list made prior to the service.]:*

The baby Jesus
Friends and family
Hugs and smiles
Laughter
Pretty flowers
Beautiful oceans
Animals
Cool breezes in the summertime
Snow in the winter
The smell of Christmas trees
Little children
Blue skies and fluffy clouds

It's okay to wish for things, but it is very important for us to realize the many gifts we have already been given. Here, I want each of you to have a copy of my "thank you" list to take with you. [*Hand out lists.*] Add to this list things you are thankful for. Sometime today, sit down and let God know how much you appreciate all of these special gifts.

*Dear God,*
*For all of the wonderful things you've given us, we thank you. Amen.*

# 6

# A Bowl of Chicken Soup

**Key Point:** We can only know true love and mercy when the burdens of others become more important to us than our own.

**Objects:** Soup bowl, spoon, and a can of soup

**Scripture:** Genesis 4:9; Romans 12:10; Galatians 6:2; Philippians 2:4.

**Preparation:** None

Hello! I'm glad to see you today. I have all of the fixins' for the perfect bowl of chicken soup: A bowl, a spoon, and a can of soup. All you need to do is open the can, pour the soup into a bowl or a pan, put the bowl in your microwave oven, or put the pan on the stove, and presto! You have the perfect bowl of chicken soup for any occasion. You're probably wondering why I've brought this soup with me today. Well, a long time ago, my sister and a bowl of chicken soup taught me a very important lesson about being a Christian.

One day, when I was in grade school, my older sister and I both had the flu. I remember lying in bed moaning from the pain in my head, sure my hair would melt because my forehead was so hot. My stomach was doing flip-flops and my bed was swaying back and forth. I was truly miserable. Sometimes between moans I could hear odd noises from the kitchen, but I was in too much pain to care what was causing them. After a while, I heard a noise outside my door. Then the door opened. Standing in the doorway was my sister with a bowl of warm chicken soup she had prepared for me. I couldn't believe it; I knew she had to be feeling as badly as I was, but she set her pain aside so she could take care of mine. She sure made me feel better.

My sister taught me a very important lesson that day—a lesson God has been trying to get across for a very long time: our love for others begins when we set our pains aside to tend to theirs.

*Dear God,*
*Give us the strength to put our problems aside so we*
*can help heal the pains of others. Amen.*

# 7

# Good Morning

**Key Point:** Every day is a gift from God and we should rejoice, for there will never be another day like this one.

**Object:** None

**Scripture:** Genesis 1:3–5; Psalm 118:24; Luke 11:3; 2 Corinthians 4:16.

**Preparation:** None

Good morning! It certainly is good to see you this morning! How many of you like getting up in the morning? [*Wait for a show of hands.*] Not too many of you. When I was a little boy, I didn't care much for mornings either. I would sleep as long as I possibly could, which, unfortunately, wasn't very long because my father would wake me each morning with a song. The song he used to sing went something like this: "Good morning to you! Good morning to you! We're all in our places with bright, shiny faces! Good morning to you!" But when I joined in, the song went something like this: "Good morning to you! 'Dad go-o-o awa-a-ay!' Good morning to you! 'Le-e-eave me alo-o-one!' We're all in our places with bright, shiny faces! 'Ple-e-ease sto-o-op!' Good morning to you! 'Okay, okay I'm up, just don't sing anymo-o-ore!'" No matter how we get up in the morning, the way we eventually greet a day is very important. Every day is different, and once a day is gone there will never be another one quite like it. So let's be thankful for each day God has given us. Let's fill each activity of our days with as much joy as we can, because once the day is done we cannot change how it was spent.

*Dear God,*
*Thank you for this day for there will never again be another one like it. Amen.*

# 8

---

# God Doesn't Make Junk

**Key Point:** God made everything for a reason.

**Objects:** Cardboard box, old shirt, broken toy truck, worn-out baseball glove, scuffed-up poster and an assistant

**Scripture:** Psalm 139:13–14; Ecclesiastes 3:11; 1 Timothy 4:4; 1 Peter 4:10.

**Preparation:** Place all of the items in the box prior to the service.

This is my friend [Corey] and I have asked him to help me with my story. Hey, [Corey], I just finished cleaning out my bedroom closet and I found all of this junk. [*Hold up box filled with "junk."*] I'm getting ready to throw it out, but I figured I'd show it to you before I did. First, I found this old ragged sweatshirt [*pull out shirt*] and . . . (Corey) "Hey, that would be perfect for wearing when I play football in my backyard. May I have it?" Well, I don't see why not, after all I was going to throw it out. [*Hand him the shirt.*] Next, I found this old truck [*pull out truck*] that I haven't played with for a long time. Look, one of the wheels is missing. (Corey) "I know a little kid down the street who has been wanting a truck like that. I don't think he would mind if a wheel were missing. Would it be alright if I took the truck too?" Sure, it's just junk to me. [*Let him take the truck.*] I also found this old beat-up baseball glove [*hold up glove*] that's too small for me now. (Corey) "I've been looking for a glove just like that one." Well, I guess you won't have to look anymore. [*Hand him the glove.*] Finally, there's this old poster I found. [*Hold up and unroll poster.*] I wouldn't hang this anywhere my friends could see it. (Corey) "Wow! I think that would look great in my bedroom. May I keep it?" Sure, take it. [*Hand him the poster.*] I guess that leaves me with this box to put in the trash. (Corey) "Well, I sure could use something to carry all of this neat stuff you've given me. May I..." It's all yours; here. [*Slide the box over to him.*] Enjoy yourself.

Well, I guess I've learned an important lesson here: what's junk to some people may be treasure to others. Sometimes we treat people like this. Just because somebody is different from us, we treat them like junk and ignore them; but remember, God thinks they are important. God made everyone for a very special reason. He made you and me. God made us, and God doesn't make junk!

*Dear God,*
*Thank you for making each of us so important.*
*Amen.*

# 9

## Jellybeans, Hugs, and Smiles

**Key Point:** The most important things we have to share with others are things God has already given us.

**Objects:** One jellybean, one hug, and one smile

**Scripture:** Ecclesiastes 5:10; Proverbs 15:30; 1 Timothy 6:10.

**Preparation:** Ask a youth or adult to assist with the story.

Hello, it's so good to see everyone today. Tammi and I have a few things we'd like to show you. These are all special things we enjoy and share with others. Tammi's holding the first item in her hand. Can you tell me what it is? (Someone should say "A jellybean.") That's right, it's a jellybean. We all like to eat jellybeans, don't we? Jellybeans are even better when we share them with friends. Tammi is now showing us something else we enjoy giving and receiving: a big smile. [*Make it a big, cheesey smile that all can see.*] I love it when people smile at me; smiles make me feel warm all over. Now Tammi and I are going to show you another thing that's great to share with others. [*Give each other a nice, warm hug*]. Mmmm . . . Boy, nothing beats a good hug. Don't you feel good now, Tammi? (Tammi) "Yeah, sure." Thanks, I do, too. Now jellybeans, smiles, and hugs all have something in common: they're all things we enjoy giving and receiving. However, one of these things is not like the others. Point to Tammi. [She eats the jellybean.] Ooops, no more jellybean. Now that Tammi's eaten the jellybean, she can't enjoy it or share it with anyone; but she still has plenty of hugs and smiles left. You see, things like jellybeans and toys and games don't last very long. Toys break, games lose their pieces, and jellybeans get eaten; but hugs and smiles are around forever. Hugs and smiles are given to us by God to share with others. God wants us to give as many hugs and smiles as we can to show everyone how wonderful his love for us really is.

*Dear God,*
*Thank you for hugs and smiles to share with everyone. Amen.*

# 10

# Getting Ready for a Birthday
## *(Advent)*

**Key Point:** The season of Advent is a time to prepare ourselves for Christ's birthday.

**Objects:** A large paper sack, helium-filled balloons, party hats, invitations, present, and a birthday cake with a candle

**Scripture:** Isaiah 40:3; Malachi 3:1–2; Matthew 3:3; John 1:23, 27.

**Preparation:** Prior to the service place all of the items in the bag. Write an invitation for each of the children, welcoming them to attend a birthday party on December 25. Purchase or make enough party hats for each child. Have some matches available to light the candle on the birthday cake. Ask someone to assist in handing out hats and invitations.

I'm so glad you are all here today, because you are going to help me get ready for a birthday party. What are some things we need to do before we can have a party? [*Allow a few responses, but move along quickly before the children get sidetracked.*] I have a few things here that will help us get ready for someone's birthday. First, we have to have people or it wouldn't be a party, would it? So, here is an invitation for each of you. [*Hand out invitations.*] Next, we'll need some fun hats! A birthday party isn't a birthday party without hats! [*Hand out hats.*] And no birthday party is complete without balloons. [*Hand a balloon to each child.*] Presents for the birthday person are a must. [*Hold up a wrapped present for all to see.*] Finally, we need a birthday cake. [*Bring out the cake and light the candle.*]

Isn't this fun? Do you think a birthday would be any fun if we didn't get ready for it? Of course not. To make a birthday special, you need to take time to get ready for it. Today we are starting a season called "Advent" which is four weeks long. During these four weeks we are preparing for a birthday. Whose birthday are we getting ready for? (Someone will hopefully say "Jesus.") That's right, the baby Jesus'. During the next few weeks we'll be sharing songs, buying presents, sending out cards and doing many wonderful things to prepare ourselves and others for a very special day: Christmas.

*Dear God,*
*We thank you for this special time of Advent to get ready for a very important birthday. Amen.*

# 11

## Plain Brown Wrapper
### *(Christmas)*

**Key Point:** God gave Jesus to us as a gift of love and we celebrate this gift by sharing gifts of love with others at Christmastime.

**Objects:** Small gift wrapped in plain brown paper and a bundle of rags

**Scripture:** Matthew 1:21; Luke 2:11–12; John 3:16.

**Preparation:** Cut out enough 1" x 2" wooden blocks for each of the children. Using a heart-shaped rubber stamp and red ink pad, decorate each block with a red heart. Wrap each block with brown paper. Take a small piece of packing string and tie a bow around the small package. Make copies of the following message for each package: "This gift of love is wrapped in plain brown paper just as God's gift of love was wrapped in swaddling clothes. This gift is not to be opened yet, but to be held until Christmas morning as a reminder of God's love for us and my love for you." Attach this message to each gift with tape or string. Have an assistant available to help hand out packages.

How many of you are getting excited about Christmas? [*Wait for a show of hands.*] Well, I know I certainly am! How do you think your presents will be wrapped this year? Do you think they'll be covered in shiny paper with pretty pictures and decorated with ribbons and bows? Do you know what these are? [*Hold up the rags*]. Yes, these are rags. Would you like to have a Christmas present wrapped in these? [*Hold up the rags and let a few give answers.*] What would you say if I told you that you already have received a present wrapped in rags? The very first gift we were given for Christmas was the baby Jesus. God gave Jesus to us as a gift of love, but instead of wrapping him in expensive blankets and fancy clothes, God had this gift wrapped in "swaddling clothes" or rags. He did this so we would understand that the importance of his gift was not in how the baby looked but in how much love the Christ child brought into this world.

I have a gift for each of you. [*Hand out packages, but remind them not to open them until after they have opened all their gifts on Christmas morning.*] There's a little tag on your gifts that I would like to read to you. The tag says, "This gift of love is wrapped in plain brown paper, just as God's gift of love was wrapped in swaddling clothes. This gift is not to be opened yet, but to be held until Christmas morning as a reminder of God's love for us and my love for you."

When you open your gifts this Christmas morning you may get "just what you wanted," or "what you needed"; your gift may be "just the right size," or "too big," or "too small." No matter what you may receive this Christmas, please remember that the real gift you are giving and receiving is love.

*Dear God,*
*Thank you so much for our gift of love wrapped in*
*rags. He is indeed the greatest gift you've ever given*
*us. Amen.*

# 12

# Remember Me
## *(Communion Sunday)*

**Key Point:** Communion is a time to remember what Jesus did for us.

**Object:** A bright ribbon tied in a bow around the index finger

**Scripture:** Matthew 26:26–29; Mark 14:22–25; Luke 22:17–20; 1 Corinthians 11:23–26.

**Preparation:** Cut enough lengths of ribbons so each child can have one to place on his/her finger. Have an assistant or two to help tie ribbons.

It's good to see you! Some of you have probably noticed I have a little ribbon tied around my finger. Why do you think I would do something like this? (Some will say "So you don't forget something.") That's right, to remind me not to forget something very important. What are some other things we do so we won't forget important things like doctor appointments or meetings? (Some suggestions might be "Write a note," "Put it on the calendar," "Tell my mother," or "Ask to be reminded.") Today we are going to have "Communion." Communion reminds Christians of a very important event. What important event are we remembering through Communion? We are remembering what Jesus Christ did for us: He gave up his life on the cross for everyone. This is a very important thing to remember. We break bread to remind us of Jesus' body which was broken when he was nailed to the cross. We drink juice to remind us of the blood he shed when his skin was torn open. I would like to give each of you a little ribbon to tie around your finger and when you look at it, think of what we are asked to remember through Communion. Then thank Jesus for what he did for us.

*Dear God,*
*Thank you for your son Jesus and all that he did for us in the name of love. Amen.*

# Someone to Take Our Punishment
## *(Good Friday)*

**Key Point:** Christ took the punishment for all of the things we do wrong.

**Object:** A big paddle

**Scripture:** John 10:10; Romans 5:8; 1 Corinthians 15:3; 1 Peter 3:18.

**Preparation:** Keep the paddle hidden in a paper sack or under a towel. The shock value of pulling out a paddle really gets their attention.

Hello! It's good to see everyone. I have something to show you. [*Pull out the paddle*]. I noticed some of you moved back a little, I guess that means you know what I am holding in my hand. What is this? (Some will say "It's a paddle.") That's right, it's a paddle. What would something like this be used for? Usually a paddle is used to punish someone when they do something wrong. Now suppose you did something wrong, and you were going to get paddled and someone you never met came up and said he would take your punishment for you. What would you think about this person? ("He's crazy!") Yes, he probably would seem crazy to be willing to do something like this, but I think it also shows he cares very much for you. You know what? Someone has already done this for all of us. Many years ago, Jesus Christ willingly took the punishment for everything we have ever done wrong or will ever do wrong. Jesus died on the cross so God would forgive us of all our sins. This was a very loving thing to do and it is very important for us to thank him for the punishment he took for us.

*Dear God,*
*Thank you for sending Jesus to take the punishment*
*for all our wrongs. Amen.*

# 14

## Preparing Ourselves for Worship

**Key Point:** It is important for us to prepare ourselves for worship by opening our hearts and minds to God's word.

**Scripture**: 2 Chronicles 29:29–30; Psalm 95:6; John 4:24.

**Objects:** A softball, baseball glove, baseball bat, baseball cap, Bible, songbook, and church bulletin

**Preparation**: Have the pastor say, "Let us open our hearts and minds and prepare ourselves for worship," at the beginning of the worship service.

This is an exciting time of the year for me because spring is coming and along with spring comes softball season! I'm a softball nut. Before the season begins, though, I thought it would be a good idea to get myself prepared. What do you think I need to prepare myself for softball? How about a softball? One of those would come in handy. [*Hold softball.*] Can you think of anything else that a person would need to play softball? A glove would be nice. [*Hold up glove.*] Yeah, I need something to look at when I miss the ball. How about a bat? Would I be ready to play softball if I didn't have a bat? Of course not. I need a bat so I can hit the ball and get on base and score runs. [*Pick up bat.*] So, here's my bat. Now if the sun is shining brightly, a cap like this one [*put cap on your head*] would be helpful in keeping the sun out of my eyes so I could see everything that's going on around me. Okay, it looks like I have everything I need to play softball, except for one thing: I have to want to play. I can get all the things I need to play the sport, but I'm not fully prepared unless I'm in the mood to play.

It's important for us to get prepared for things like softball and other sports, but how do we prepare ourselves for worship? Would a Bible help? [*Hold up Bible.*] Yes, we need to have a Bible. How about a songbook? [*Hold up songbook.*] We need songbooks so we can sing our songs to God. [*Pick up bulletin.*] This bulletin helps us to follow what's happening during the service. With all of these things in hand, do you think we are prepared to worship? I'd have to say "No." At the beginning of the service, the pastor said something that is important to do before we can be fully prepared for worship. He said, "Let us open our hearts and minds and prepare ourselves for worship." You see, we can have our Bibles, and our songbooks and our bulletins, but unless we decide we want to worship God, and learn about his word, then all these things aren't worth much. Let's prepare our hearts and minds now:

*Dear God,*
*We love you and we want to learn how to be good*
*Christians. Please be with us as we open our hearts*
*and minds and prepare ourselves to worship you.*
*Amen.*

# 15

# The Red Bible

**Key Point:** The Bible becomes a great book only when we read it.

**Object:** A red Bible

**Scripture:** Deuteronomy 17:19–20; Psalm 119:105; Revelation 1:3.

**Preparation:** None

I have a little red Bible with me. It reminds me of a little boy who once had a red Bible. This little boy received a red Bible as a gift and he was very proud of it. He took it to Sunday school and church every Sunday. When the preacher read the Scripture lesson during worship, he would read along in his red Bible. Yes, he was very proud of his Bible. One Sunday the minister said something in church that made the boy very happy. The preacher said the most important Bible is a "red" Bible. Well, the boy was so proud of his Bible now that he began bragging to the other children in church that his

Bible was more important than theirs because his was a red Bible. He would say "The preacher says I have the most important Bible because mine is red! Ha, ha, your Bibles aren't as important as mine!" The minister happened to overhear the boy's words and asked him, "Why do you think your Bible is more important than anyone else's Bible?" The boy replied, "Because you said the most important Bible is 'red' and mine is red." "My son," the pastor said, "I'm afraid you misunderstood. I said the most important Bible is one that is well read. Your Bible is not important unless you read it."

The lesson this little boy learned is one we should learn, too. Our Bibles do not become important books unless we read them. We need to read God's word often so we can learn how to be the special people he wants us to be. Make your Bibles important today.

*Dear God,*
*Thank you for all of your wonderful words in the Bible. Help us make these words important to us by reading our Bibles often. Amen.*

# 16

## Plenty of Love for Everyone
### *(After Thanksgiving)*

**Key Point:** Our bodies were made so we can never give nor have too much love.

**Scripture:** Joel 2:26; Romans 12:1; 1 Corinthians 13:1–3, 13.

**Object:** None

**Preparation:** None

Hello! Did everyone have a nice Thanksgiving? Did you watch all of the colorful parades on television? How many of you ate a lot of food? [*Wait for a show of hands.*] Did anyone have pumpkin pie? How about cranberry sauce? Stuffing? I'm sure most of you ate plenty of turkey. Our bodies can only take so much turkey, stuffing, pies, and cranberry sauce. God made us so we can only take so much of just about anything. He made us so we can work only so long. He made us so we could play only so hard. As a matter of fact I can think of only

one thing God made that we can't have too much of
and that's love. He made us so we can never have or
give too much love. Maybe God is trying to tell us
something here. He wants us to share as much love
as we possibly can in our lives. We share our love by
being friendly, caring, patient, kind, and by *not*
being selfish, jealous, angry or boastful. Be sure you
share some love today.

*Dear God,*
*Please help us share as much love as we can. Amen.*

# 17

# Showing We Are Christians

**Key point:** Even though we may say we are Christians, we show people we are Christians by our love.

**Objects:** A can of corn and large label (resembling a food can label) made of butcher paper and cardboard

**Scripture:** Leviticus 19:18; Deuteronomy 10:19; Matthew 22:32–40; John 15:17.

**Preparation**: Remove the label from the can of corn by cutting along the seam of the label with a knife or razor blade. Carefully remove the label without tearing. Cut out a 3' x 4' piece of butcher paper and print on it the word *Christian*. To reinforce the paper, cut out a piece of cardboard the same size and tape or glue the paper to the cardboard. Tape the ends together so you have a large tube that will fit over a small child. Take some time to make it look like a product label; this adds to the effectiveness of the object.

It's good to see everyone today. What do I have in my hand? [*Hold up the can without a label.*] That's right: a can. What do you think might be in this can? [*Allow some time for a few suggestions.*] Well, if this can had a label on it we would have an idea of what is inside, wouldn't we? I have an extra label right here. [*Hold up the label for all to see, then place it on the can.*] This label says this is a can of corn. So apparently, there is corn inside this can. How many of you believe this label is telling us the truth? [*Ask for a show of hands.*] Well, there's only one way we can know for sure there actually is corn inside, and that would be to open the can and look at its contents.

Let's try something else now. Ronnie, would you please come and stand beside me? [*In advance, get the child's permission to help.*] Ronnie is a Christian, but how can he let everyone know that he is a Christian? Hey, we could put a label on him like the one on this can of corn. I have a "Christian" label right here. [*Place label over the child.*] Now will everyone know Ronnie is a Christian? We weren't real sure there was corn in this can and it has a label. You know, there's really only one way Ronnie or any of us can let people know we really are Christians and that's by showing them. Just saying we are Christians isn't good enough; it's very important we show others we are Christians by being the loving and caring people God wants us to be.

*Dear God,*
*Please help us to show others how much we love you*
*by loving them. Amen.*

# 18

# God Is Everywhere

**Key point:** God is everywhere and even if we cannot see him we can see all of the wonderful gifts he has given us.

**Object:** An inflated balloon

**Scripture:** Psalm 16:8; Matthew 28:19–20.

**Preparation:** Inflate the balloon before the service. You will also need a needle or other pointed object to burst the balloon.

Hello! It's good to see all of you today. I would like to show you something that I brought to church with me. [*Hold up the balloon.*] What do you think is inside this balloon? Air? How do you know there is air in this balloon? Can you see it? [*Turn balloon slowly so the kids can see all sides.*] Let's try a little experiment. I brought a needle with me and I'll burst the balloon with it. Look closely when the balloon pops and tell me if you can see the air inside. [*Burst the balloon.*] Did anyone see the air? I sure didn't, but we all know there was air in the balloon or it wouldn't have been so round and pretty.

The Bible tells us that God is everywhere, but can we see him? No we can't, but we know he's there. Just as we knew there was air in the balloon, because it was round and pretty, we know that God is all around because of all the beautiful things he's given us. Flowers and trees tell us that God is near. The wonderful friends in our church family are examples of God's being with us. No, we can't see God, but we can see all of the gifts he's given us and that's very special.

*Dear God,*
*Thank you for all of the wonderful gifts that con-*
*stantly remind us that you are near. Amen.*

# 19

## God Is Not a Fireman

**Key Point:** God is not around just for emergencies; he's around to share our lives.

**Object:** A fireman's helmet

**Scripture:** Isaiah 55:1–2; Psalm 3:3–4; Matthew 11:28; Luke 11:2–4.

**Preparation:** Get a helmet from a local fire station or purchase one from a local department store.

Hello! It's wonderful to see so many of you! Does anyone know what this is? [*Hold up helmet so all can see.*] ("It's fireman's hat.") That's right; it's a fireman's hat. What are some things firemen do? ("Put out fires." "Save people." "Get kittens out of trees.") Yes, firemen help with all types of emergencies. Sometimes people treat God like he's a fireman. The only time they talk to God is when they need his help. God is not a fireman; he's much more. There are many stories in the Bible that tell of people talking to God for a lot of different reasons. There are times when people ask God to help them out of tough situations; but these people also share their joys with God. They tell God when they are sad. People in the Bible tell God when they are happy and when they are angry. No, God is not a fireman. God's our friend and he wants us to share our entire lives with him.

*Dear God,*
*Thank you for being our friend. Amen.*

# 20

# A Wonderful World
of Many Colors

**Key Point:** God made us different on the outside to make the world a more exciting place to live; and he made us all different on the inside so we could make the world a better place to live.

**Object:** Jar of M&M's

**Scripture:** Psalm 34:14; Philippians 4:7; 2 Peter 1:5–8.

**Preparation:** None

It's good to see all of you! I have a jar full of M&M's. Look closely at this jar and tell me how many different colors you see inside. ("Green." "Brown." "Red." "Yellow." "Tan." "Orange.") Why do you think the people who made this candy gave it so many different colors? Do the colors have different flavors? ("No.") Well, do you want to know why I think they gave the candy different colors? I think they did it to make the candy more exciting and more fun to eat. However, we don't eat M&M's for the outside do we? ("No.") No, we eat them for their insides. What is inside of the colored coating? ("Chocolate!") The color on the outside makes M&M's more exciting, but the most important thing about the candy is the chocolate inside.

God made people different colors. He made black people and red people; white people and yellow people. He did this to make the world a more exciting place to live. The earth would be a pretty boring place if we all looked the same on the outside. However, just like M&M's the most important thing about people is not what they look like on the outside, it's what God gave them on the inside. He gave us each a heart to love with and a mind to think with. What we look like on the outside makes the world a more exciting place to live. What we do with our insides can make the world a better place to live.

*Dear God,*
*Thank you for making the world an exciting place to live. Please help us to make it a better place to live. Amen.*

# 21

---

# Shine for God

**Key Point:** Anger, guilt, and junky feelings keep us from being able to share God's love with others.

**Object:** A flashlight filled with nuts, bolts, assorted junk, and batteries

**Scripture:** 2 Chronicles 30:9; Ezekiel 36:25–26; James 1:19–20; 1 John 1:9.

**Preparation:** Fill the flashlight with nuts, bolts, etc. before the service. Have some batteries for the flashlight available. Have a bowl to empty the flashlight's junky contents into during the story.

It's nice to see you. I've brought this really neat flashlight to show you. Here, let me turn it on . . . [*Turn switch off and on a few times.*] Hmmm . . . There seems to be something wrong with my flashlight. Let's take a look inside and see what's the matter. [*Open flashlight.*] No wonder this thing wouldn't work. [*Pour contents of flashlight into bowl.*] There's no way this flashlight could shine with all of this junk inside. [*Put in batteries.*] Let's see what happens now. [*Turn flashlight on and shine it back and forth to show that it now works. Turn flashlight off and set it down.*]

You know, we're like this flashlight. Sometimes we have junk inside of us that makes it hard for us to shine for God. We might have junky feelings inside such as anger, guilt, or jealousy that keep us from being the people God wants us to be. We need to get rid of that junk so we can shine for God. The only way to do this is to ask God to take these feelings away and forgive us for having them. When we do this God takes away the junk inside of us and replaces it with love and forgiveness so we can shine in his love. Do this often so you can always shine for God.

*Dear God,*
*Please take away all the junky feelings inside us so we can shine for you. Amen.*

# 22

---

# The Proof of a Thumbprint

**Key Point:** God loves us so much that he gave us our own thumbprint.

**Objects:** An ink pad, an index card, and a thumbprint

**Scripture:** Deuteronomy 7:9; Psalm 91:14; Ephesians 2:4–7.

**Preparation:** Have a paper towel handy to wipe the ink off your thumb.

It's good to see all of you today. I would like to tell you how much God loves you, but before I do this, I'd like you to do something for me. I'd like you to turn your hands over like this [*Turn them palms upward.*] Now I want you to look at your fingers very closely. Do you see all the little squiggly lines on the tips of your fingers? These make up your fingerprints and the ones on your thumb make up your thumbprint. Watch me. [*Roll thumb on ink pad and make a thumbprint on the index card.*] This is a copy of my thumbprint. There is no other thumbprint exactly like mine in the whole world. God loves me so much that he made my thumbprints and fingerprints different from everybody else's. He did the same for you. Nobody has thumbprints or fingerprints exactly like yours. God loves you so much that he took the time make you different from everybody else in a special way. Isn't that great! God loves you, and you have the thumbprint to prove it.

*Dear God,*
*Thank you for our thumbprints; they show that you love us very much. Amen.*

# 23

# Choices

**Key Point:** God gives us the freedom to choose to do good things or bad things.

**Object:** A pocket knife

**Scripture:** Deuteronomy 30:19; Joshua 24:15; John 7:17.

**Preparation:** None


Hello! It's nice to see everyone! I have something in my pocket; let me get it out . . . [*Remove knife, but don't open it.*] Do you know what this is? ("A pocket knife!") That's right, it's a pocket knife. Now let me open it for you . . . [*Open knife.*] What are some helpful things we can do with this knife? ("Carve a piece of wood." "Peel a potato." "Get a splinter out of your hand.") Yes, these are all good ways to use a knife. What are some bad things we could do with this knife? ("Hurt someone." "Scare people with it." "Cut ourselves.") Yes, these are things we shouldn't do with a knife.

People are a little like knives; they can do both good and bad things. What are some good things people can do? ("Hug someone." "Help someone who is in trouble." "Make people smile.") Yes, these are all good things people can do for one another. What are some bad things people can do? ("Hurt someone." "Yell at each other." "Steal.") Yes, these are all bad things people can do. As I said before, people are like knives; they can do good things and they can do bad things. There is, however, one big difference between people and knives: People can choose whether or not to do good or bad things, knives cannot. God gives us the freedom to choose our actions. When we choose to do good things, we choose to follow what God wants for us. When we choose to do bad things, we choose to go against what God wants for us. When you think about the choices you have to make, choose to follow God.

*Dear God,*
*Please help us make the right choices. Amen.*

# 24

# Helping Harold

**Key Point:** We not only need to wish for things to be better, we also need to make things better for those around us.

**Object:** A dying plant and a book

**Scripture:** Micah 6:8; Philippians 4:9; 1 John 3:17; James 2:16–17.

**Preparation:** None

This is my friend Harold. [*Hold up plant.*] Now, I'm sure many of you have noticed Harold is a plant. Don't you think Harold looks a little brown? I don't think he's feeling too well today. I sure hope he starts feeling better soon. Maybe some water and sunlight would help him. I hope he gets these things. I hear plants grow better if you say kind words to them. Somebody better say some nice things soon, because Harold really isn't looking too good. A bigger pot might help. I hope someone gives him one. I have something else with me. [*Hold up book.*] It's a book about taking care of plants. Maybe it can tell us who can give Harold all the things he needs to get better. [*Open book.*] It says here "To help a sick plant you must water it, and give it lots of sunlight. You need to talk nicely to it often. If the pot is too small, you should put the plant in a bigger pot." So, if Harold is going to get any better, someone needs to do all these things. The book says "you" must do all of these things and that means me. I'm the one who should help Harold. I'm glad I looked at this book or I would have never known I was the one who was supposed do all of these things for Harold.

We need do the same thing for people. We look at those who are hurting and say, "I hope someone makes them feel better." We see people who don't have enough food to eat and say, "I sure hope they get something to eat soon." It's nice to hope things would be better for those around us, but if we were to look in the Bible, we would see God wants us to do things to help hurting and hungry people. We should care, and hope, but also help.

*Dear God,*
*We do hope things in this world get better, but please give us the strength to help where we can. Amen.*

# 25

# Mom's Comforting Arms
## (Sunday prior to Halloween)

**Key Point:** God is always there to comfort us in time of need.

**Object:** A plastic mask

**Scripture:** Joshua 1:5; Matthew 28:20; John 14:1.

**Preparation:** None

[*Place mask up to your face*] Boo! Did I scare you? Have you ever been so scared that your face turned white, your eyes bugged out, and your hair stood straight up on end? Well, I haven't either, but I've been close. I remember one time in particular: One dark Friday night when I was eight years old, my sister and I were lying on our sofa watching a scary movie. My older brother and his friend, who was spending the night, were goofing around in the back bedroom. Mom came into the television room and told my sister and me that my brother and his friend were planning on scaring us. Then she sat down and put a comforting arm around each of us. A little time had gone by, and my sister and I had forgotten all about the scare attack planned for us. We were curled up next to my mom watching this scary movie. About the time we thought everything was safe, my brother and his friend came running and screaming into the room. They had put some junk all over their faces that made them look really spooky. They scared the "bajeebers" out of me. When this happens your arms and legs go flying all over the place; and the only word you can get out of your mouth is "Aaaah!!!" Well, I finally calmed down after my brother and his friend left the room laughing and patting each other on the back for a job well done. At first I was angry with my mom for letting them scare me so badly. I wondered why she didn't tell them to stop. I blamed her for not being there when I needed her the most. Why had she abandoned me like that? But then I realized she still had her arm around me and was hugging and kissing me, she had never left my side. I got so frightened that I forgot she was there. If I had just taken the time to realize she was there for me, I probably wouldn't have been so scared.

Have you ever been so worried about something you think no one cares and no one can help you? Well, I'll let you in on a little secret: God cares and he's always there for you. The next time you get scared or worried: stop, be calm, and know that God is there with his comforting arm stretched around you.

*Dear God,*
*Thank you for caring and for being there whenever we need you. Amen.*

# 26

# Christmas in July
## (For a Sunday in July)

**Key Point:** The gift of love we celebrate at Christmastime is something to celebrate all year.

**Object:** A Santa Claus hat

**Scripture:** Matthew 2:9–11; Luke 2:9–11.

**Preparation:** None

Merry Christmas! What? This isn't Christmastime? Well, I guess you're right; Christmas is a few months away. You know, Christmas is probably the most important holiday we have. On Christmas day we celebrate the birth of Jesus Christ by exchanging gifts with those we love. On the day of his birth, Christ brought love into this world. This is definitely something worth celebrating, but why not celebrate this love all year round? We can celebrate Christmas today. We can celebrate Christmas in July by bringing cans of food to our food pantry. We use this food to give to people in town who don't have enough to eat. We can celebrate Christmas in July by wrapping presents and giving them to the people at the nursing home down the street. We can celebrate Christmas in July and every month of the year by sharing with others the gift of love given to us on the very first Christmas day. The birth of Christ is something worth celebrating in December, and July, and every other month of the year.

*Dear God,*
*Thank you for the baby Jesus, your gift of love to us on Christmas day. Be with us as we celebrate this gift in July and every month of the year. Amen.*

# 27

# Make Time for God

**Key Points:** It is important for us to set time aside each day to talk with God and invite him into our lives.

**Objects:** Paper sack, two videotapes, a small radio, a box of crackers, a football, a book, and a Bible

**Scripture:** 2 Chronicles 15:2; Jeremiah 29:13; Matthew 7:7–8; Acts 17:27.

**Preparation**: Have all of the items on the floor beside the sack prior to the sermon.

Boy, do I have an exciting day ahead of me! Here in front of me I have everything I'm going to do today. I'm going to put everything in this sack that I've made time for today. Okay, first I think I'll watch a couple of movies. [*Place tapes in the sack.*] Next, I think I'll listen to some music. [*Place radio in sack.*] Oh, and I can't leave out my afternoon snack. [*Put box of crackers in the bag.*] After I finish my snack, I'll call up my friends and we'll play football.

[*Place football in the box.*] I also have this book I want to read. [*Place book on top of the sack.* At this point, the bag should be full.] Finally, I have God . . . uh, oh, it looks like I didn't set any room aside for God today. Well, that's not good. God has done so much for me; he helps me with all of my worries and troubles. I don't think I could go through a day without taking time to tell him how much I appreciate him and need him in my life. I'll just take a few things out and make time for God today. This is something we all need to do. Sometimes we get our days so full of work or fun that we forget to make time for God. He wants us to have all these things, but he also wants us to talk with him each day. Take some time today and every day to talk to God and tell him how much you appreciate all he's done and ask him to be with you in all that you do.

*Dear God,*
*Thank you for being so wonderful to us, please be with us today in our work and play. Amen.*

# 28

---

# Trapped by Impatience

**Key Point:** God wants us to be patient.

**Object:** Chinese finger trap

**Scripture:** Isaiah 30:18; Proverbs 14:29;
Hebrews 10:36; James 5:7–8.

**Preparation:** Practice getting fingers out of
the trap prior to the service.

It certainly is nice to see all of you today. Today I
have brought something very interesting to show
you. [*Hold up finger trap.*] Does anyone know what
this is? ("A Chinese finger trap!" or "Finger-cuffs!")
That's right, this is what I've come to know as a
Chinese finger trap. Apparently, some people think
if you put a finger in each end of this gadget [*Put
the forefinger of each hand in opposing ends of the
trap*] it will trap you, but I don't believe this. [*Tug on
the trap a couple of times.*] Well, it does seem to
work. Oh, I know; all I have to do is hold it at an
angle like this. [*Raise one hand higher than the other*

*and tug.*] Hmmm, that doesn't seem to work. How about if I were to hold it above my head. [*Hold hands above head and tug, then start getting visibly frustrated over your dilemma.*] Now this is getting silly, I need to hurry up and get out of this thing so I can get on with my lesson. [*Begin flinging hands back and forth as if your frustration is increasing.*] I'm getting fed up with this contraption . . . Aaah!! [*Give up and lay hands in lap.*] You know what? I think I'm doing this all wrong. If I were to slow down and be patient, all I would need to do to get out of this trap would be to press down on one end like this, [*Press forefingers toward one another so the trap bulges in the middle. Push down on one end of the trap with the thumb and middle finger. The forefinger should slip out without too much effort*] and then with the other finger [*Repeat the process.*] I think the individual who invented this little gadget knew people pretty well. The inventor probably knew people like to get through with most things as quickly as they can and that's the secret to this trap. You see, you get trapped with impatience. The faster you try to get out, the more trapped you get.

The importance of being patient is something God wants you to understand. Sometimes you get impatient to do as much in a day as you can. You get home from school and try to finish your homework [*speed up as the list lengthens*], watch your favorite show on television, call your best friend on the phone, and go to your baseball game all before bedtime and when you can't get it all done you get so frustrated eventually you just go "Aaah!" You get angry and usually do something you regret like pull your sister's hair, kick the dog, or upset mom and dad. God doesn't want this to happen. He wants you to be patient and do things one at a time. God is always with you and there's nothing coming your way that you and God can't handle.

*Dear God,*
*Please help us to be patient. Amen.*

# 29

# Remember Daddy
## *(Father's Day)*

**Key Point:** It is important for us to remember all of the things our fathers have done for us.

**Objects:** A hammer, storybook, baseball glove, car keys, and a Bible

**Scripture:** Joshua 4:4–7; Exodus 20:12; 1 Thessalonians 2:10–11.

**Preparation:** Place all items in a paper bag or small box prior to the service.

Hello! Does anyone know what day this is? ("Father's Day!") That's right; it's Father's Day and I have a special message for you on this occasion. First, I would like to tell you a Bible story. This story is about a man named Joshua. Joshua was trying to get the Israelites across the Jordan river, but they could not cross, because the water was too deep. To help Joshua, God parted the waters of the Jordan, and the Israelites safely walked across the river's bottom. When all of these people were safely across, Joshua asked twelve men to gather one large stone each from the river bottom. The stones were then stacked at the edge of the river to serve as a reminder to the Israelites and their ancestors of what God had done for them that day. The story tells us it is important to remember what God has done for us; but we should also remember what those people God has put in our lives have done for us as well. Especially our fathers. Just as Joshua's men gathered up stones, I have gathered up a few special items which remind me of what my father has done for me. This hammer [*hold up hammer*] makes me think of all the neat things my dad helped me build. We made boats, little cars, slingshots, and even a footstool for my grandfather. When I was your age, my father would read me a story every night before I went to bed. He was the world's greatest storyteller. I have this storybook to remind me of those special times. [*Place book on pile.*] Dad taught me how to play baseball, football, and a lot of other sports, but baseball was my favorite. [*Place baseball glove on the pile.*] Whenever I had trouble doing my homework, especially math, Dad was always willing to help. This schoolbook reminds me of those times. [*Place book on pile.*] These car keys are to remind me of all the times Dad helped fix my car when it broke down. [*Place keys on top of pile.*] When you get older you'll understand how important it is to have a car that works. Finally, I have this Bible. My father has always shown me how important it is to have God in my life. [*Place Bible on top of pile.*] Take some time today to remember what God has done for you and let him know you appreciate these gifts. Then take some time today to remember some of the things your father has done for you and thank him for all he's done.

*Dear God,*
*Thank you for our fathers and all they have done for us. Amen.*

# 30

# Sharing God's Secrets

**Key Point:** We learn secrets about God's love every week in church, but these are secrets God wants us to share with everyone.

**Object:** A treasure map

**Scripture:** Exodus 18:20; Deuteronomy 4:9; Matthew 10:27; John 4:40–42.

**Preparation**: Roll up the treasure map and wrap a piece of string around it prior to the service.

It's good to see all of you today. Do you know what I have in my hand? [*Hold up the map.*] I can't tell you because it's a secret. (Singing) "I've got a secret and I'm not gonna te-e-ell you!" (*Pause.*) Oh, okay, how many of you would like to see what I have? [*Wait for a raise of hands.*] All right, I'll show you, but you can't tell anyone. [*Unroll the map.*] This is a treasure map that shows where a treasure chest is buried very close to this church. Apparently, a pastor who really liked kids buried this chest full of toys, games, candy, and money a long time ago. Now you know my secret, but remember, you can't tell anyone. I'm just teasing, there really isn't a treasure; but if this were a true story, how many of you would like to tell someone about this treasure? [*Wait for a show of hands.*] Yeah, it would be hard to keep a secret this big to yourself.

Every Sunday we learn a lot of secrets about God that many people don't know. In the Bible there are stories about Jesus doing amazing things like making blind people see, and deaf people hear, and curing others who had terrible diseases. We also find stories about love and forgiveness. In church we learn the meaning of these stories. These are indeed wonderful secrets we learn every Sunday morning, but they are not secrets we should keep to ourselves. These are special things God wants us to share with as many people as we can. Share a secret about God today.

*Dear God,*
*Thank you for all of your wonderful secrets. Please help us to share them with as many people as possible. Amen.*

# 31

## You're Invited

**Key Point:** We are invited to follow Jesus in our daily lives.

**Object:** An invitation to follow Jesus

**Scripture:** Deuteronomy 10:12–13; Psalm 119:105; Matthew 16:24; John 14:6–7.

**Preparation:** Make copies of invitations to be given to the children. Have an assistant available to help hand out invitations.

It's good to see so many of you! I would like to read a story out of my Bible. [*Open Bible and invitation falls out.*] Ooops! What's this? It says on the front it's an "Invitation." Wow! I wonder what I'm getting invited to. How many of you have ever received an invitation? [*Wait for a show of hands.*] What kinds of things do you get invited to? ("Birthday parties!" "Christmas parties." "School parties.") Well, I've been invited to weddings, graduations, baby showers and many other special occasions. I wonder what special event I'm getting invited to with this invitation. Well, I'll wait until after church to open it up and find out. Let's get back to the Bible story I was going to read . . . Hmmm. . . . [*Begin turning pages in the Bible as if looking for a certain passage, but too preoccupied to continue the pursuit.*] Oh, I can't stand it, I have to know what's inside this envelope. Would you like to know? ("Yes!") Okay, I guess I'll open it then. [*Open invitation and read to yourself.*] Hmmm . . . Wow! This is really neat! How many of you like to get invitations? [*Wait for a show of hands.*] This invitation is from Jesus to all of us. It says:

> *Dear Child of God:*
>
> *You are invited to be my disciple. You are invited to live a life of obedience, love, kindness, forgiveness, and understanding. If you should accept this invitation, you will receive life everlasting. Please let me know your reply today in your prayers.*
>
> *Love, Jesus Christ*

Every day we are given a special invitation from Jesus Christ to follow him and show everyone how wonderful God is. Would you like to accept this invitation? If so, tell Jesus. I have an invitation like this for each of you. [*Hand out invitations.*] Read over the invitation and tell Jesus you would like to follow him.

*Dear God,*
*Help us to accept Christ's invitation to follow him.*
*We know it's very important to you. Amen.*

76

# 32

# A Happysad Day
## *(Palm Sunday)*

**Key Point:** Palm Sunday is a day to remember the happy and sad moments of the last week of the life of Jesus Christ.

**Object:** A "Happysad" face

**Scripture:** Matthew 21:8–9; Mark 11:8–10; Luke 19:28, 36–37; John 12:12–13.

**Preparation:** Take a 10" paper plate and fold it in half. On one side of the plate, draw half of a smiling face. On the opposite half of the plate, draw half of a frowning face. Unfold the plate and you should have a "happysad" face.

Today is Palm Sunday, and I have a "happysad" face to help me wish you a "happysad" day! [*Hold up face.*] If you look closely, you'll notice half of this face is smiling and the other half is frowning. This is because today is both a happy and a sad day. Palm Sunday is a happy day because we remember today as the day when Jesus entered the city of

Jerusalem and people crowded all around him and cheered. They put palm leaves on the ground for him to walk on so his feet wouldn't get dirty. Some folks even took off their robes and laid them on the ground for him to walk on. Palm Sunday is a happy day because so many people were happy to see Jesus. Palm Sunday is a sad day because we know in the week which followed, Jesus suffered a great deal. He was betrayed, put on trial, beaten, and put on a cross to die. But Palm Sunday is a happy day because we know in exactly one week (three days following his death) Jesus came back to life and is with us now and forever. So you see, Palm Sunday is a "happysad" day!

*Dear God,*
*Be with us today as we celebrate Palm Sunday, a "happysad" day. Amen.*

# 33

## It's a Miracle
### *(Easter)*

**Key Point:** The miracle of Christ's resurrection is indeed a miracle worth celebrating.

**Object:** Copy of the pastor's sermon notes

**Scripture:** Matthew 28:5–7; Mark 16:6–7; Luke 24:6–8; John 20:1–2.

**Preparation:** Make a photocopy of the pastor's sermon notes.

Hello! Does anyone know what day today is? ("Easter!") Yes, it's Easter Sunday! I have something really fantastic to show you for my lesson today. Before I can show you, I need a sheet of paper . . . [*Look around for a piece of paper.*] Hmmm, I seem to have forgotten to bring some paper with me. Hey, I saw the pastor carrying some paper into the sanctuary this morning, let's see if he can loan me a sheet. [*Turn to the pastor.*] Pastor, do you have a sheet of paper I could borrow for a minute? (Pastor) "Well, I have my sermon notes." That will be perfect. [*Take notes from pastor.*] I'll give them back when I've finished. Don't worry, they'll be perfectly safe. [*Take the sheet and act like you're looking over the notes.*] Hmmm . . . you're really going to tell them all this? Oh, well, they might buy it. Anyway, the reason I need this sheet of paper is to show you something incredible I saw a magician do on television last week. He took an ordinary piece of paper like this and folded it in half.

[*Fold the paper in half.*] Then he folded it again. [*Fold again.*] Finally, he ripped it in half. [*Rip the paper.*] (Pastor) "He what?" Don't worry, everything will be all right. Then the magician ripped the paper again. [*Rip again. Look as if you're beginning to enjoy yourself.*] Next, he took these bits of paper and stuffed them into his hand and said a magic word. [*Stuff paper into a loosely closed fist, then cup other hand over the fist and say "Hocus, pocus!"*] When the magician said these words, guess what happened inside his closed hand? A miracle happened! All the bits of paper grew back together just like this [*Open hand and let little pieces of paper fall out of your hand to the floor.*]. Ooops! I guess we'll be having a shorter sermon today. You know what, I don't think this was a miracle at all, I think the magician tricked me.

Well, this may not have been a miracle, but there is one miracle I know really happened. Many years ago Jesus Christ was put up on a cross. His body was broken and his blood spilled. After Christ died they put him inside a tomb, a small cave in the side

80

of a hill. They put a large rock in front of the entrance of the tomb. The body of Christ was in that cave for three days; but on the third day a miracle happened! God brought Jesus back to life. Because of this miracle, we know Jesus is the Son of God and is with us now and forever. This is indeed a miracle worth celebrating, and that's what we do every Easter.

*Dear God,*
*Thank you for bringing Jesus back to life. It is a miracle worth celebrating. Amen.*

# 34

## Fix It, Daddy
### (Earth Day)

**Key Point:** The earth was given to us as a gift from God and we need to take care of it.

**Objects:** Tree seedlings

**Scripture Reference:** Genesis 1:26–29, 9:1–3.

**Preparation:** Purchase enough seedlings for each child. Some nurseries may donate them. Arrange to have someone help hand out seedlings.

It's nice to see all of you today. How many of you have ever received a special gift that you didn't take care of and eventually it broke? [*Wait for a show of hands.*] And after you broke this gift, how many of you took it to your father and said "Fix it, Daddy"? [*Show of hands.*] Well, I did this many times when I was your age. As a matter of fact, I still do it sometimes. I'm sure occasionally, after your dad would fix your gift, he would say, "You know you need to take care of this or someday you may not have it anymore." Have any of you have heard this warning? I certainly have.

Many years ago, God gave the earth to us as a gift. He gave us all the animals, oceans, lakes, skies, and forests to care for. Through the years we have not taken good care of our gift. As a result of our carelessness, some of the animals we were given are not here anymore, the oceans are full of trash, and our forests are being cut down. Today, many people are taking their concerns for our planet to God, saying "Fix it, Daddy." God's response to these prayers is probably, "I'll do what I can, but you need to take care of this gift or you may not have it much longer." We need to start taking better care of the earth or we may not have some of the wonderful things we now enjoy very much longer. There are a lot of things we can do to make our planet a better place to live. We can pick up trash, save aluminum cans, and plant trees. When we plant a tree we make our air cleaner to breathe, we help our soil stay healthy, and we give animals a place to live. I have brought a little tree for each of you to plant. [*Hand out seedlings.*] Take care of God's gift to us and tell others to do the same.

*Dear God,*
*Thank you so much for giving the earth to us. Please help us to take care of this gift so we never lose it. Amen.*

# 35

**Be Trustworthy**
*(Boy Scout Sunday)*

**Key Point:** God wants us to be worthy of the trust of others.

**Object:** A Boy Scout

**Scripture:** Exodus 18:21; Daniel 6:4; Luke 16:10–12; Titus 1:7–9.

**Preparation:** None

Today is Boy Scout Sunday and to help me with my lesson are two Boy Scouts, Steven and Zach. I have asked these two to help me recite the Boy Scout Law. The Scout Law is a list of rules Boy Scouts are expected to follow every day. Okay, guys, let's give it a try:

> A Scout is...
> Trustworthy
> Loyal
> Helpful
> Friendly

Courteous
Kind
Obedient
Cheerful
Thrifty
Brave
Clean
and Reverent.

These laws are very important to the Boy Scouts. If you noticed, this list began with the word *Trustworthy*. It is very important that a scout is worth trusting. You've probably seen in cartoons where a Boy Scout eagerly helps a little old lady cross a street. The important lesson here is a scout can be trusted to help with such a task. I think this is a very important law for Christians as well. If you say you are a Christian, people should be able to trust you to be loving, caring, forgiving, and understanding. Christians should be trustworthy.

*Dear God,*
*Help us to let others know they can trust you because*
*they can trust us. Amen.*

# 36

# Take Care of Mother
## *(Mother's Day)*

**Key Point:** Mother's Day is a time to take care of our mothers.

**Object:** None

**Scripture:** Deuteronomy 5:16; Proverbs 20:11; John 19:26–27; Ephesians 6:1–3.

**Preparation:** None

What is today? [Mother's Day!] That's right, it's Mother's Day. I've got a little quiz for you today. Can you think of some important mothers mentioned in the Bible? ("Eve." "Noah's wife." "Mary.") Very good. There are a lot of mothers mentioned in the Bible, but I think the most important one is Mary, the mother of Jesus. Jesus loved his mother very much. When he was dying on the cross he looked down and saw Mary standing next to his friend and disciple, John. In all his pain and suffering, Christ looked at John and said, "Take care of my mother." Not too long after this, Jesus died.

I think Christ gave us a very important message in his last moments on the cross. Our mothers have done a lot for us out of love, and we need to take good care of them. Today is a special day for mom. I think we need to follow Jesus' example and make sure our mothers are taken care of today. After our prayer, I'd like you to go back to your seat and give your mother a hug. Give your mom lots of hugs today; it's a special day just for her.

*Dear God,*
*Thank you for our mothers, they are very special.*
*Amen.*

# 37

# Threads of Faith

**Key Point:** We are stronger when we gather together to do God's work.

**Objects:** A strand of thread, a group of threads twisted together, and a brick

**Scripture:** Ezra 3:1–3; Psalm 102:21–22; Matthew 18:20; 1 Corinthians 5:4–5.

**Preparation:** Cut about twenty strands of sewing thread approximately 10" long. Set one strand aside and twist the remaining threads together and tie a knot on either end to keep them from separating.

Hello! It's good to see you! Does anyone know what this is? ("It's a thread.") Yes, it's a piece of thread. There are lots of things you can do with a piece of thread. You can sew up a hole in your pants and you can hold a button on your shirt; but do you think I can pick up this brick with a thread? [*Hold up brick for everyone to see.*] How many of you think this thread can hold the weight of a brick? [*Wait for a show of hands.*] Well, let's give it a try. [*Stick the thread through the top hole of the brick.*] Watch your feet, I wouldn't want this brick to fall on anyone's toes. Okay, here we go! [*Lift up on the thread. The thread should break without lifting the brick.*] (Snap!) Well, what do you know, the thread didn't even budge the brick. What do you think would happen if we put a whole bunch of threads together? Do you think we could lift the brick then? ["Yes!"] I have some threads bunched together; let's see what they can do to this brick. [*Repeat the process. The threads should hold up the brick without any problems.*] Where one thread failed, many threads together succeeded.

Just like a single thread, one Christian is limited in the things he or she can do. Where one Christian can love just so many people, a lot of Christians gathered together can love people all over the world. When we gather together as Christians, we become strong. It's important for us to come to church every Sunday so we can be strong for God.

*Dear God,*
*We thank you for a place where we can gather to-*
*gether and be strong in your love. Amen.*

# 38

# I Love You, Teddy

**Key Point:** Our actions should match our words.

**Objects:** A teddy bear, a book, and a photograph.

**Scripture:** Romans 2:13; James 2:14–17; 1 John 2:6, 3:18.

**Preparation:** None

I have brought my friend Teddy with me today. Teddy is very special to me. He's my buddy and I really care about him. [*Carelessly toss the bear behind you.*] Okay, I also have brought my favorite book to show you. This book is so neat; it's full of exciting stories. I take very good care of this book. [*As you are speaking begin flipping through the pages of the book. Carelessly rip one of the pages out.*] Whoops! I accidently ripped a page. Oh, well. [*Toss the book aside.*] I also wanted to show you this photograph. [*Hold up picture.*] This is one of the best pictures I've ever taken. It's a wonderful photo of some of my friends. Hmmm . . . [*Examine the photograph.*] There seems to be a smudge on the front of the photograph. [*Crumple up the picture and toss it aside.*] Oh, well, I'll just have to find another one to show you.

Am I confusing you? ("Yes!") My words and my actions aren't the same, are they? I say these things are important to me, but am I treating them like they are important? ("No!") No, I'm not. I'm tossing them, and tearing them, and crumpling them up. Sometimes we do the same thing to people. We say we care about them, but we don't treat them like we do. As Christians it is important that our words and our actions go together. If we say we love others we should act like we love them.

*Dear God,*
*Please help us to remember our words of love aren't*
*worth much if our actions don't say the same thing.*
*Amen.*

# 39

# Practice, Practice, Practice

**Key Point:** Saying we are Christians does not make us Christians, we must practice our faith every day.

**Objects:** Flute and a flute player

**Scripture:** Deuteronomy 30:15–16; Luke 9:23; Philippians 4:9.

**Preparation:** None

It's nice to see all of you today. This is my friend Melissa. She's going to help me with my story. I have decided I want to start playing the flute today. I've asked Melissa if I could borrow her flute and she was nice enough to let me. [*Hold up flute for everyone to see.*] Would you like to hear me play? ("Yes.") Okay, here I go. [*Hold flute to lips and make a couple unsuccessful attempts at making music.*] Ohhh, I can't play the flute. Just saying I want to play the flute isn't good enough; I would have to practice. If I were to practice every day, I might be

able to play like this: [*Ask Melissa to play the flute.*]
Wasn't that pretty?

Being a Christian is a lot like playing an instrument. Just saying we are Christians doesn't make us Christians, we must practice every day. A person does not become a Christian by saying, "I want to be a Christian." A person must practice by loving and forgiving others. A person must practice by reading the Bible and trying to understand God's word. Practice being a Christian every day.

*Dear God,*
*Be with with us as we practice our faith and try to be*
*the best Christians we can be. Amen.*

# 40

# He Loves Me

**Key Point:** God does not play games with his love for us. God always loves us.

**Object:** A daisy

**Scripture:** Zephaniah 3:17; Jeremiah 31:3; 2 Thessalonians 2:16–17; 1 John 4:19.

**Preparation:** None

Hello! It certainly is nice to see all of you! I brought a daisy with me to help with my lesson. I'm sure all of you know a little game we play with flowers. The game goes like this: "She loves me [*pluck a petal*], she loves me not [*pluck another petal; continue process until petals are gone.*] She loves me, she loves me not. She loves me, she loves me not. Oh, boy! [*Pluck the last petal*] She loves me!" Being the silly kind of folks we are, we often play games with our feelings. Sometimes we say "I'll be your friend as long you don't . . . " or "I'll like you unless . . . " or "If you really love me, then you will. . . ." God doesn't do this and doesn't want us to do it either. If we were to play the same game with God's love, all we would need to do is pick the whole flower [*grab the stem and snap it in two*] and say "He loves me." God loves us no matter what we do. He would like us to do the same for each other.

*Dear God,*
*Thank you for loving us so much. Please help us to*
*follow your example. Amen.*

# 41

## Listen to the Coach
### *(Super Bowl Sunday)*

**Key Point:** We can't play the game of life very well unless we listen to the coach.

**Objects:** A whistle and a football

**Scripture:** Psalm 48:14; Isaiah 30:21; John 14:6; 1 Peter 2:21.

**Preparation:** Put the whistle around your neck and hold the football in your hands during the lesson.

Can anyone tell me what big event is going to take place today? ("The Super Bowl!") That's right! Later on this afternoon, two of the country's best professional football teams will play against one another to determine who is number one. All across the world people will sit in front of their televisions and watch some of the best quarterbacks, running backs, receivers, and linebackers run up and down a field for two hours. There are many things that must work right for a team to win this game. Good players are very important, but the most important person in the game is the coach. The coach knows all the plays and understands the opponent. No matter how good the players are, they know they won't play their best and aren't likely to win unless they listen to the coach.

Life is like a football game, except we're the players and God is the coach. We play the game of life best when we listen to the coach. Listen to God, read the Bible, and ask for his guidance every day.

*Dear God,*
*You are our coach, please help us to play the game of life as well as we can. Amen.*

# 42

# Jack and the Pumpkin Patch

**Key Point:** We feel better when we share.

**Object:** A pumpkin

**Scripture:** Isaiah 58:10; Matthew 25:34–40; Luke 6:38; 2 Corinthians 9:7.

**Preparation:** One thing you can do to make the story more colorful is choose names of people in your congregation and put their names in place of the characters in the story.

I have brought a pumpkin with me today, because it reminds me of a story about a boy named Jack who wanted a brand new bike. Jack went to the richest man in town, Mr. Bucks, and asked, "Mr. Bucks, do you have any work I could do to earn enough money to buy a bike?" "No," replied Mr. Bucks, "I'm afraid I don't, Jack. I tell you what I can do for you though, go into my pumpkin patch and pick the biggest pumpkin you can find." "Well, what good will a pumpkin do me?" Jack asked; "I want a bike!" Mr. Bucks replied, "You could take the pumpkin down to Mr. Featherstone's market and he might buy it from you." "Okay, I guess that's better than nothing." Jack put the pumpkin in a little red wagon and pulled it all the way to Mr. Featherstone's store and called to him: "Mr. Featherstone, would you like to buy this pumpkin from me?" "Sorry, Jack," replied the grocer, "I can't afford to buy any pumpkins right now. If you would like to give me your pumpkin, I could carve a face on it and decorate it and put it in my window. I think it would make everyone feel good to see a smiling face as they walk by." Jack looked at Mr. Featherstone with a frown and said, "No, I'm not interested in making people feel good. I want money to buy a bike." "Well, I can't give you any money for it," Mr. Featherstone said. "Maybe Mrs. Smith, the baker, would buy the pumpkin to make some pies." Jack turned and said, "Okay, I'll give it a try." He entered the bakery and asked Mrs. Smith if she would like to purchase his pumpkin. "No," said Mrs. Smith, "But if you would like to give me the pumpkin, I could bake some pies and give them to poor people who don't have enough to eat." Frustrated, Jack replied, "I'm not interested in feeding the poor; I want money to buy a bike!" "Well, I'm sorry I can't help you Jack," Mrs. Smith said thoughtfully. "Why don't you ask Mr. Withers what you can do with your pumpkin. He's the wisest man in town." "Well, I guess he's my last hope," Jack grumbled, as he walked away dragging his pumpkin behind. Mr. Withers lived at the top of a large hill outside of town. Pulling a big pumpkin up such a hill was quite a task. Jack finally made it to the top and knocked on the front door of Mr. Withers' house. After a few moments, the door opened and Jack said, "Mr. Withers, I'm trying to sell this pumpkin to get enough money to buy a bike. What should I do?" Mr. Withers thought for a moment and said, "I'm not sure who would buy it, but if you were to give it to Mr. Featherstone, he could carve a face on it, decorate it, and put it in the front window of his store. I think a smiling pumpkin would make people feel good." "I'm not interested in making people feel good," Jack said angrily, "I want a bike!" As if he hadn't heard Jack, Mr. Withers continued, "You could also take the pumpkin to Mrs. Smith and she could bake some pies to give to the poor." Jack replied, "I don't want to feed the poor! I want a bike!" Mr. Withers shook his head sadly and said, "I'm sorry, but I can't help you, Jack." Then Mr. Withers turned and shut the door. As Jack was struggling to get his pumpkin back down the hill, the wagon's handle slipped from his hand. The wagon zoomed down the hill and ran into a large rock, sending the pumpkin high into the air. The pumpkin landed with a loud "Splat" and pumpkin pieces were scattered all over the side of the hill. Jack returned home, knowing he would not get his bike. One year later, Jack returned to the hill and was surprised to see pumpkins everywhere. He realized these had grown from the seeds of his pumpkin. Jack saw lots of smiles as people picked pumpkins and carved funny faces on them. He saw how happy the poor were when Mrs. Smith brought them freshly baked pumpkin pies. Jack decided sharing his pumpkin with others made him feel much better than having a bike. He learned a very important lesson that day: When we share what we have with others we are much richer than if we were to keep everything to ourselves.

*Dear God,*
*Please help us to remember how important it is to share. Amen.*

# 43

# Letters from a Friend

**Key Point:** The Bible is full of letters from our friend Jesus, who constantly tells us he loves us and we are important to him.

**Objects**: Pile of greeting cards and letters and a shoe box

**Scripture:** Matthew 28:18–20; Luke 15:4–7; John 14:1–4, 10:14–15.

**Preparation**: Place some greeting cards in a shoe box or similar size cardboard box.

I'm glad you are all here today. How many of you have a friend or relative that lives far away in another city? [*Wait for a show of hands.*] Since you don't see them very often, you probably get a letter or card once in a while from these people saying how much they miss you and hope to hear from you soon. How many of you have received a card or letter recently in the mail? [*Wait for a show of hands.*] Every time I get one, I put it in this box. I do this because some days I get lonely and I like to read some old letters to remind me that somebody really cares about me. Here, I'll read one for you. [*Read a card.*] Did you know you have a collection of letters like these? Yes, we all do. They're in four books of the Bible called the Gospels. And they are full of letters from our friend, Jesus Christ. In these letters, Jesus tells us he loves us, we're important to him, and he hopes to hear from us soon. These letters are wonderful and are meant to be read by each one of us. So whenever you get the chance, pick up your Bible and read these letters from Jesus. He really does care about you.

*Dear God,*
*Thank you for all the wonderful letters from Jesus. It's nice to be reminded how important we are to you. Amen.*

# 44

# I Don't Like You, But...

**Key Point:** God doesn't intend for us to be able to like everyone, but he does expect us to try to love everyone.

**Object:** Letter about Billy

**Scripture:** Leviticus 19:34; Deuteronomy 10:19; John 15:17; Romans 12:10.

**Preparation:** None

It's good to see all of you today! I have a letter to read to you about a boy who isn't too fond of another boy named Billy. The letter goes like this:

"I don't like Billy. He says the dumbest things and he never wears the right clothes. I don't like Billy. His hair is too short and he sounds goofy when he laughs. I don't like Billy. I don't like Billy for lots of reasons, but mostly I don't like Billy because he doesn't like me."

Isn't it silly how we sometimes play games with the word *like*? I remember a game I used to play with my mother. I would go up to her and say, "Mommy, I don't like you." She would frown and say in a sad voice, "You don't?" "No," I would reply, "I love you!" Then she would smile, hug me, and I would smile and hug her back. We both won at that game. To be honest, I really didn't like my mother sometimes. Especially after she punished me for being bad. Of course, I probably deserved to be punished, but I didn't like my mother for giving me the punishment. She probably didn't like me too much either for being bad. No, sometimes I didn't like my mother, but I have always loved her, and I know she has always loved me. As Christians, we are asked to "love one another." God doesn't intend for us to always be able to like people, but he does expect us to always try to love them.

*Dear God,*
*Please help us to remember to love one another.*
*Amen.*

# 45

# Making Your Hands Strong

**Key Point:** The most important thing we can do with our hands is pray.

**Objects:** One right hand and one left hand

**Scripture:** Jeremiah 29:12; Job 22:27; Mark 11:24; John 15:7.

**Preparation:** None

I have some very interesting things to show you: I brought these! [*Hold up hands.*] There are some very special things you can do with your hands. You can play games with them. Sometimes when I get bored I like to twiddle my thumbs. [*Twiddle.*] I'm sure most of you have played this game. You can also tell jokes with your hands. [*Hold up one finger, wiggle it, and move as if it were flying past your face.*] Do you know what this is? Me either, but here comes a whole flock of them. [*Repeat this process with all of your fingers wiggling past your face.*] You can tell a story with your hands. This is the church.

[*Clasp your hands together. Have all fingers folded so they are palm-side down.*] This is the steeple. [*Point forefingers up, touching parallel to each other.*] Open the doors and here's all the people. [*Open hands, turn palms upward and wiggle fingers.*] You can also sing songs with your hands. I'm sure all of you have sung "Itsy, Bitsy Spider." You put your fingers and thumbs together like this [*put right forefinger on left thumb and left forefinger on right thumb*] and then you sing: "The itsy, bitsy spider climbed up the water spout . . . ". [*Move fingers upward in climbing motion by releasing bottom forefinger and thumb, pivoting on the other pair, and then retouching thumb and forefinger.*] Well, that's all of the song I know, but I think it's pretty neat. There are lots of things we can do with our hands, but there is one thing that is more important than all others. The most important thing we can do with our hands is put them together like this [*Fold hands, as in prayer*] and pray. When we invite God into our lives our hands are truly strong because God is guiding them. With God guiding them there are so many wonderful things we can do with our hands. Let's make our hands important right now. [*Have all the children put their hands together.*]

*Dear God,*
*We invite you into our lives to guide our hands to do your work. Amen.*

# 46

# This Is Just Grape Juice
## *(Communion Sunday)*

**Key Point:** We break bread during communion to remember Christ's body which was broken when he was nailed to the cross; and we drink juice to remember his blood which was spilled when the nails pierced his flesh.

**Objects:** Loaf of bread and a communion tray filled with cups of grape juice

**Scripture:** Matthew 26:26–28; Mark 14:22–24; Luke 22:19–20.

**Preparation:** Set communion tray and loaf of bread in front of you prior to the children's story.

Hello! It's nice to see all of you! Today is communion Sunday, and I have some of the things we use in communion [*point to tray and bread*], but before I say anything about them, I would like to tell you a little story. I was helping a pastor serve communion one Sunday morning. As I stood with the communion tray in front of a boy about five years old, the pastor said, "Take this as Jesus' blood which was spilled for you." Well, when he heard the preacher's words, the boy's eyes got real big and he started looking around to see what everyone else was doing. Then he slowly reached up and took one of the cups from my tray and drank from it. He quickly turned to his mother who was sitting beside him and said, "This is just grape juice!" He was right; this is just grape juice, but it is also much more than that. We take this bread [*hold up loaf*] and break it to remember that Christ's body was broken when they nailed him to the cross. We drink this juice [*hold up tray*] to remember that Jesus bled when the nails tore his skin. Jesus Christ suffered a great deal because he loves us. We have communion to remember what he did and to thank him for loving us so much. Remember this is much more than just grape juice and this is much more than just bread. Remember what Christ did for us and thank him.

*Dear God,*
*Thank you for your Son and the pain he went through because he loves us. Amen.*

# 47

# The Good Gym Teacher

**Key Point:** God wants us to love our neighbors, even the ones we don't like.

**Object:** None

**Scripture:** Leviticus 19:18; Proverbs 3:29; Matthew 19:19; Romans 13:8–9.

**Preparation:** None

It's nice to see all of you today. A long time ago Jesus told his followers, "Love your neighbor." When a man asked, "Who is my neighbor?" Jesus told a story similar to this one: Once upon a time there was a boy playing on the playground. He was minding his own business, bouncing a red ball up and down. Not paying attention to where he was going, the boy wandered onto a part of the playground where only the mean kids played. Suddenly, some of these mean kids came and threw the boy on the ground and stole his ball. When the boy tried to get up and chase after them, he realized he couldn't stand because his knee was cut and bleeding. He sat there crying for a long time, and then he saw the principal walking his way and the boy thought, "Great! He'll help me!" But the principal, afraid the mean kids might come and push him down too, crossed to the other side of the playground and kept walking. A little time went by and the boy's homeroom teacher came walking his way. The boy thought, "Surely, she'll help me. I'm her best student." The teacher, having the same fears as the principal, also crossed to the other side of the playground and kept walking. The boy had given up all hope of someone helping him off the playground, when he saw the gym teacher walking his way. "Well, he certainly won't help me," thought the boy. "He's mean and always makes me do sit-ups for chewing bubble-gum in class. Last week he sent me out in the hall three times! There's no way he'll help after all I've done." To the boy's surprise, the gym teacher walked right up to him, picked him up and carried him to the school nurse's office. Then the gym teacher helped the nurse clean the boy's wounds and called his parents to come and take him home for the rest of the day.

The man asked Jesus the question, "Who is my neighbor?" The answer to this question is "everyone." In spite of the fact he and the boy did not care much for one another, the gym teacher set his own feelings aside and helped the injured child. God wants us to be like this, to love everyone, even those we don't necessarily get along with.

*Dear God,*
*Help us to be like "The Good Gym Teacher" and set*
*our feelings aside so we can love all our neighbors.*
*Amen.*

# 48

# Reminders

**Key Point:** Even though our sins are forgiven we will always be reminded of our actions.

**Object:** A mixer

**Scripture:** Job 11:13–15; Psalm 147:3; Acts 10:43; Colossians 2:13–14.

**Preparation:** None

Do you know what sin is? You sin when you do something you know you shouldn't do and you do it anyway. I've brought this mixer with me to help me teach you a little lesson about sin. When I was a boy, I used to enjoy helping my mom make cakes. I enjoyed this for several reasons, but one of the biggest was that I could use the mixer. I really got a kick out of watching those beaters spin round and round. One day I started poking the beaters with my fingers while the mixer was running. My mom saw what I was doing and said, "Don't do that or you'll get your fingers caught." I said, "Okay," but as soon as she turned away I started doing it again and guess what happened: The mixer went "Rrr!" and my finger was caught between the beaters. It really hurt and the only word I could get out of my mouth was "Ah, ah, ah. . . ." Mom turned around, shook her head in disgust and pulled the beaters apart so I could get my finger out. My finger was bleeding and I begged forgiveness. I said, "Mom, I know I shouldn't have done it and I'm sorry." She said it was okay and took me into the bathroom, washed off my finger and put a bandage on it. Even though my mom forgave me for disobeying her, I still have a little scar on my finger to remind me I did something wrong. God forgives us when we sin, but we need to remember even though we are forgiven there will always be things to remind us of what we've done wrong. These reminders may be physical like the scar on my finger, or they may be broken friendships, hurt feelings, or lost trust. We must try very hard to avoid doing what we know is wrong.

*Dear God,*
*Please help us to avoid doing what we know is wrong because we know even though we are forgiven we leave reminders behind. Amen.*

# 49

# Pay Attention

**Key Point:** We need to pay attention in church or we may miss something very important.

**Object:** A picture with objects hidden in it

**Scripture:** Proverbs 4:1; Isaiah 42:20; Romans 10:17; Hebrews 2:1.

**Preparation:** These pictures can be found in various children's magazines.

It's good to see everyone today. I have with me a picture. This is not an ordinary picture. If you look closely, you'll find several hidden objects. For example, if you look closely at this tree, you'll notice there is a hammer hidden in its trunk. [*Point to outline of the hammer.*] Can anyone find something else? Yes, there is a boot hidden in this rock. [*Point to outline of boot.*] Do you see anything else? Well, I see a cup hidden here in the grass. [*Point to outline.*] We could go on, but I think the preacher has a sermon this morning, so we'll stop here. If you were to try to find all of the items hidden in this picture, you'd have to pay close attention or you might miss something really neat. Worship is the same way. Everything we do during worship helps us to learn about how God wants us to live as his disciples. If you don't pay close attention to what's going on, you might miss something very important. Pay attention in church today and every Sunday. If something happens that you don't understand, ask your parents to explain it to you. If they don't understand, then ask the preacher; and if *he* doesn't understand, then ask me and we'll figure something out. Anyway, pay close attention during worship so you can learn as much as you can about being the wonderful person God wants you to be.

*Dear God,*
*Thank you for this place and the wonderful people we gather with to learn your ways. Amen.*

# 50

# We Care

**Key Point:** When we pray in church, we are telling God, "We care."

**Objects:** People in the congregation who are hurting

**Scripture:** Jeremiah 37:3; Colossians 1:9; 2 Timothy 1:3; James 5:16.

**Preparation:** None

Hello! It's good to see all of you! We're going to try a little experiment today. We have friends in church who are hurting. Some people are worried about a family member who is ill, some are not feeling too well themselves, and some have other pains that are troubling them. Whatever the reason, these people are hurting and need someone to care about them. Why don't we tell them, "We care." Let's just have one of us tell these hurting people, "We care." [*Pick one child to say, "We care."*] Okay, now let's try with three of us saying it together. [*Pick three differ-*

ent children to say, "We care."] Good, now how about all of us telling them how we feel. (Everyone says, "WE CARE!") Wow, that sounded great. When do you think these people really knew we all cared about their pain? (Someone will say, "When we all told them.") Yes, when we all said, "We care." The same thing happens when the preacher stands up and says, "Would you please bow your heads for a word of prayer." When he does this, he is asking each of us to bow our heads and help him tell God, "We care" about everything in the prayer. So this morning when the pastor asks you to bow your heads for prayer, instead of looking at the ceiling, or poking the person next to you, or looking around to see how many other people are looking around, bow your head and listen to what he is saying and help the pastor tell God, "We care." It means so much to God and to those we are praying for when we do this.

*Dear God,*
*We care about all of the people who are hurting.*
*Please help ease their pain. Amen.*

# 51

# Love Your Enemies

**Key Point:** When you love an "enemy" you
may wind up making a friend.

**Object:** None

**Scripture:** Proverbs 16:7; Matthew 5:44; Luke
6:27–28, 34; Romans 12:20.

**Preparation:** None

It's nice to see all of you today. How many of you
have heard a verse from the Bible that tells us to
"love our enemies?" [*Wait for a show of hands.*] This
is a hard thing to do, but many years ago I found
out why Jesus told us to do this. When I was in ele-
mentary school, I had a teacher I didn't get along
with too well. I upset her, nearly every day. One day,
my teacher called my parents and asked them to
meet with her to discuss my classroom behavior. After
talking with her my parents told me they were disap-
pointed in the things I had done. They asked me why
I was so discourteous to my teacher and I answered,
"Because I don't like her." "Well, why don't you like

her?" they responded. "Because she doesn't like me!" I exclaimed. Then my mother said, "Give us a minute to think about this." I knew I was in big trouble now. After a short discussion, my parents returned and presented my punishment. "To get on better terms with your teacher, we think you should invite her to one of your baseball games this week." "Whoa," I thought, "Anything but that. I'd have to actually talk to her on the phone like a normal human being. Then I'd have to invite her to be a part of the most important activity in my life." Well, I called my teacher on the phone and said, "Uh, hello, this is Kyle Godsey, I'm one of your students." She said she knew who I was and I continued, "Well, I was wondering if you'd like to come and watch me play baseball this Thursday." "Why certainly! I'd love to!" she replied excitedly. Not only did my teacher attend my baseball game that Thursday night, she came to every one of my games for the remainder of the season. I remember her sitting up in the stands yelling, "Let's go, Kyle!" every time I got to bat. All this support came from someone I had once considered an enemy. Somehow our relationship turned completely around and instead of an enemy I had a new friend. This came as a result of my parents asking me to take a risk and open my life to her. It certainly was a lot harder on me to hate her than to love her. Jesus told us to "love our enemies." He asks us to do this because in our enemies we may find very good friends.

*Dear God,*
*Please help us to love our enemies, they might make*
*good friends. Amen.*

# 52

# Spanking Boy

**Key Point:** Jesus Christ willingly took the punishment for our sins so we wouldn't have to take the punishment ourselves.

**Object:** A storybook about some kind of royalty

**Scripture:** Romans 5:9–10; 1 Corinthians 15:3; 2 Corinthians 5:14–15; 1 Thessalonians 5:9–10.

**Preparation:** None

Hello! It's good to see all of you! I have a book with me that tells a story about a prince who traded places with a pauper (or poor person) who looked just like him. The prince wanted to see what living a normal life was like. [*Hold up book.*] How many of you have read stories about kings, queens, princes and princesses? [*Wait for a response.*] Who were some of the people these stories were about? ("Sir Lancelot," "King Arthur," "Beauty and the Beast," "Cinderella.") Very good. How many of you have heard the story about the "Prince and the Pauper"? [*Hold up book and wait for a show of hands.*] Do any of you know what a spanking boy is? Well, long ago, whenever a prince did something wrong, it was against the law for anyone to punish him. Since the prince couldn't be punished, a person called the "spanking boy" was given the honor of taking the prince's punishment, which sometimes was a spanking. Believe it or not, this was a position many young boys wanted. It was considered an honor to be a spanking boy. Wouldn't it be nice to have our own spanking boy to take our punishment when we do something wrong? Guess what? We *do* have a spanking boy and his name is Jesus. Jesus was glad to be our spanking boy. When he died on the cross, Christ took our punishment for everything we've ever done wrong or will ever do wrong. Because of Jesus' sacrifice, God forgives our sins. Isn't that wonderful! This is something all Christians should remember and be thankful for. Christ is our spanking boy: He took the punishment for our sins so we wouldn't have to take the punishment ourselves.

*Dear God,*
*Thank you so much for giving us Jesus to take the punishment for our sins. Amen.*

# Scripture Index

(Numbers in bold refer to lesson number, not page number.)